SCHIRMER'S LIBRARY
OF MUSICAL CLASSICS

Vol. 1987

Claude Debussy

Twelve Etudes

For Piano

ISBN 978-0-7935-3158-5

G. SCHIRMER, Inc.

DISTRIBUTED BY

HAL•LEONARD®
CORPORATION
7777 W. BLUEMOUND RD. P.O. BOX 13819 MILWAUKEE, WI 53213

CONTENTS

TWELVE ETUDES
for the piano

Claude Debussy

I.   for the "five fingers" in the manner of Mr. Czerny

II. in Thirds

III. in Fourths

IV. in Sixths

V. in Octaves

Joyous and carried away, rhythmically free

A Tempo
in ritmo uniforme, senza affrettare

(con sordino)

rinf. poco //

rinf. poco //

pp

pp

u.c. sempre, Ped. on each beat

simile

pp

pp

pp

VI. for Eight Fingers *

Vivamente, molto leggiero e legato

*In this étude, the use of the thumb is made awkward by the changing position of the hands. To use the
thumb in performing this étude would require the pianist to be an acrobat.*

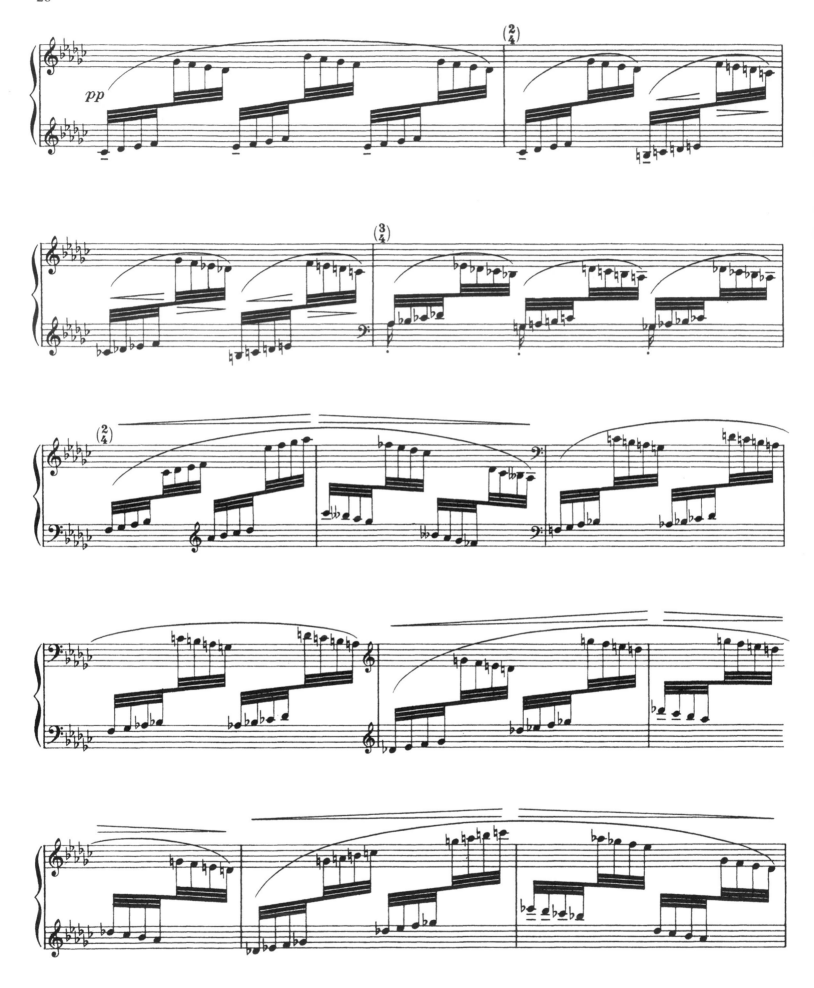

the low notes slightly espressivo

VII. in Chromatic Half-Steps

Scherzando, animato assai

VIII. for Ornaments

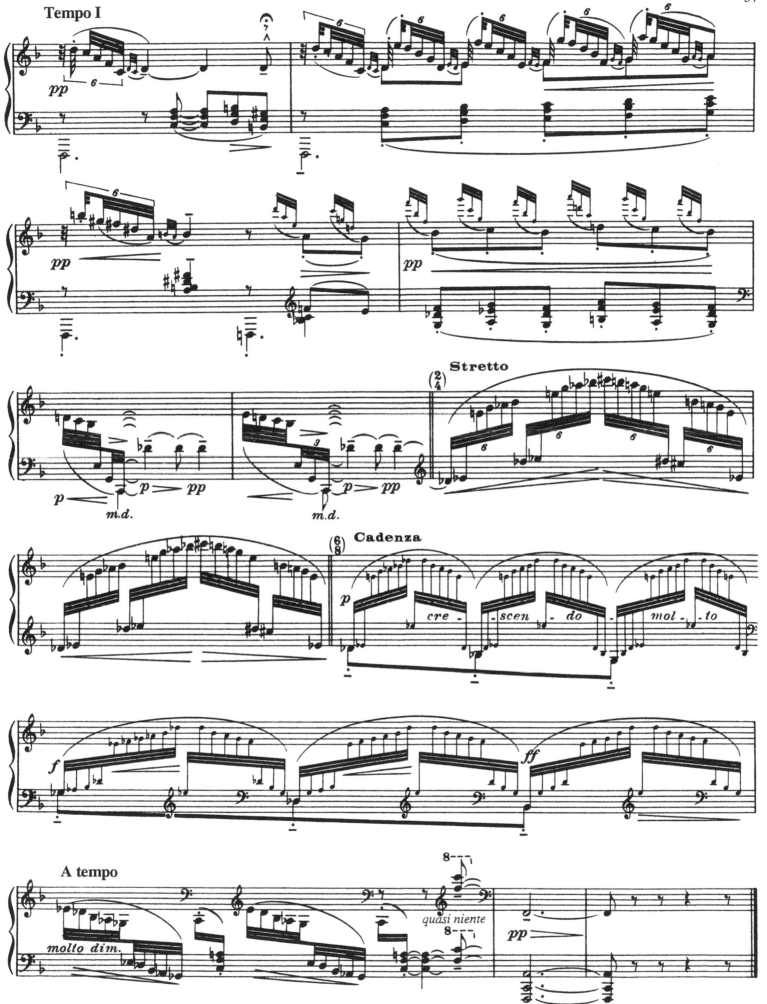

IX.　for Repeated Notes

X.   for Contrasted Sonorities

Moderato, ma non troppo

XI. in Compound Arpeggios

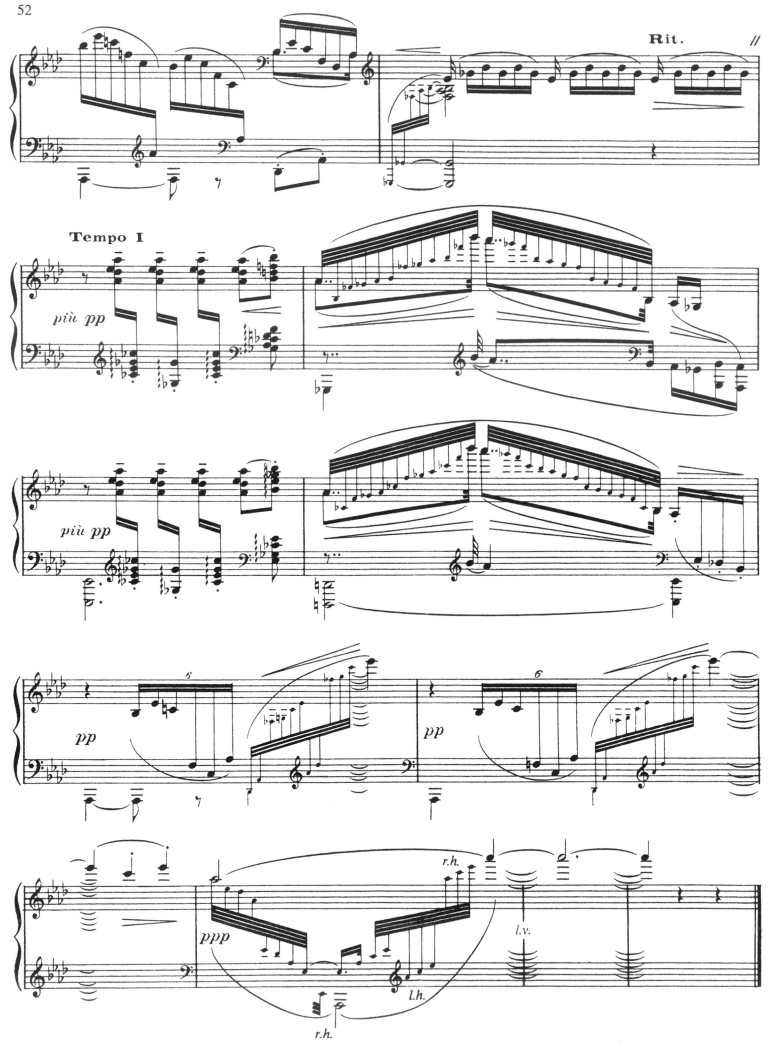

XII. in Chords

Deciso, ritmico, non pesante